TO JANAYA ♥

you
are
safe
here.

thank you
for giving these
little pieces of
my heart a home.

♥AVA.

AVA.

ISBN-10: 1530335175
ISBN-13: 978-1530335176

*oh, the heartbreakingly beautiful
tender weight of being human.*

this is for me
and this is for you.

lover,
you are allowed to feel how you feel.
i have built this safe space for you.
  you no longer have to be afraid;
  no one can hurt you here.

    you are free
      to let yourself be.
      to let yourself fall.
      to let yourself heal.

you will
find the meaning in your pain.

to be
brave.

i just want to be
honest about my feelings
without destroying everything.

the opening,
the breaking,
the falling apart
    is always so quick.

the hurting,
the healing,
the putting back together
    is always too long.

my words have feelings.
i need you to read them.
i need you to know what they mean.

i am a body
that carries sadness
as if it is the only thing
that belongs there.

i forget that love
and warmth
and peace belongs there too.

and sadness clung to me
because she did not know
how to be alone.

inside me,
i am large.

i contain infinities,
contradictions,
currents
and
hurricanes
of
love
and
fear.

there is no end
inside me.

what is this need to please?

where did i learn to apologize
   before i speak?

   when will i learn to love
      without giving myself away?

sometimes,
i would place a hand over my chest
   and leave it there,
close my eyes and feel the slow beat.

i think if i listened hard enough,
i will know what it wants,
   and why it throbs,
      and how it bleeds.

as if all i had to do was be still
   and it will tell me everything.

i am finding myself.
i am allowed to take my time.

i do not take.
i give.
i only love.

i am a bleeding heart.
i am open arms.

i do not know how to be anything
   other than this.

i over love.
i under love.

i am either
a flood

or i am nothing.

i can't hold onto love.
i'm not gentle enough.

i always end up
crushing the thing
in between my fingertips.

i do not know how to accept love
even though i keep giving it away.

i keep throwing it into people's faces,
begging them to take it—

begging them to take
all of it away.

everything i know about love
is that it hurts
and is almost always never returned
the way you want it to.

but i have hope
because i do not know everything.

i'm lying here
on the black top,
getting soul fried
by the sun.

     i'm waiting for it to rain.
     i'm waiting for the leaves to change.

     i'm waiting for everything.

i feel like i'm missing something.
i feel like i'm on a plateau with no end.

i am numb
and i'm marinating in mediocrity.

where is my life experience?
my grand adventure?
how can i jump off this cliff?

where the fuck is the goddamn edge?

i'm ashamed at how soft i exist.

how much my life
is lived without me,

how much my breathing
feels more like fading,

how much my heart gives
and never takes.

i am.

i am too much myself
and this is too much for you,
but in my truth,
i am free.

i act harder than i am.
i am softer than i look.

i felt my love
too deep,
complicated,
untranslatable,
unstable,
unrealistic,
too broken
for you.

i am shy.
i don't like being seen for my looks,
it never comes out well.
i want you to see me for me.
for who i am.
maybe, for who i'll become.
see something in me i won't see.
see something more
than just this body and flesh.

i've become afraid of people touching me
who do not love me.
i'm afraid of what they want.

i'm more afraid of how little they want,
and that my heart can no longer survive
that kind of touch.

i am too much.
i have always been too much.

you open the door
and i am the pill you cannot swallow.
you shut the door, but it's too late.

i spill and i am spilling. i overflow.
  i overfill. i over love. i over flood.

if you want me,
be sure to want me,
before it's too late.

my heart is everywhere.
my heart is everywhere you touch.
do you understand?

do you understand
why i cannot let you touch me?

do not let anyone in
until they love you so fiercely,
you have no defense against their love.

you have been careless with your body.
you have left too much of you behind.

call all the pieces of you home.
collect them like flowers in your hands.
see how beautiful you are
   when you are altogether.

you were uncomfortable.

you ran to colder bodies
—to whiskey warm words,
found new comforts that meant nothing.
you began to think of life as a series of
    discomfort. discontent. dis—ease.
your body is tired of being emptied
    into lesser things.

remember when your grandmother used to
    rub menthol and eucalyptus oil
        into your belly?
rub oil into your belly again.

let the warmth
    gather into all the places that ache.

feed your body, honey and lemon.
make your mother's favorite tea.
keep the leftover leaves for the smell.
remind your body of home,
    where it came from.
remind your body of how it was loved
    before you chose to chase after ghosts—
    things you imagined in your head
        to be so real,
    you abandoned home
            for a phantom of a feeling.

go outside.
find a flower and tell it you love it.
find a place to put all the love
that has become heavy and hard to carry.
remind yourself that
this is what being alive feels like—
    a sharp stab of joy.
    a soft lingering of pain.

remind yourself
    how it used to be easy to breathe.
remind yourself it can be easy again.

it is there—
    at the end of your sadness,
    at the end of your weariness,
   nestled deep inside
    your cradle of bones—

       your bed of clouds,
       your crown of flowers
       your secret peace
         to lay rest
         your too soft soul.

crush red flowers
    into a powder
    into your hands.
imagine it is your heart
    finding a way to be lighter.
extend your arms
    as if you were giving a gift to the sky.
let the wind carry
        all the pieces of your heart away.

trees grow thick with love
and then
they change.

love
and
love
and
love
until
you're
so
full
of
love,
that
you

break.

you have outgrown this skin.
stop trying to hold it in.
stop trying to hold it together.

let yourself break.

let the stars inside you breathe,
before the darkness swallows them whole.

let them burn through your skin
and light this whole goddamn world on fire.

this is the growth
that is meant for you.

this is your becoming.

you are allowed to
take up all the space
you need.

you are allowed to
fill in all the corners
and flood the room.

don't stop
until you are done.

you wanted it all to make sense
and you wanted the most complicated answer,
but the answer is simple.

just be.

your wounds are where
   your father was wounded.
your bitterness is the life
      your mother had to live.

and if we do not
   do something different,
these wounds will be
      the wounds of our children,
      who we hope,
            will learn how to forgive.

i think we're all saying the same thing,
   but in our own way.
i think we just need to learn
   to listen to each other.

we shun things that are not like us.
we want to put them in boxes and
stack them neatly into packages of
understanding, but none of us are
meant for the boxes placed before us.

we spill over and join one another
   at the edges, leaning forever
   towards something more.

i will never understand why we attack people
that are different from us.

why are we so afraid of something
we don't know?

why do we approach people with fear
instead of love?

why do we insist on holding onto prejudices
rather than onto each other?

remember
you are capable
of the most powerful thing
in the universe.

you are capable of love.

you're going to love your way
out of this.
   out of the hurt.
   out of the pain.

you're going to love your way
   out of it and be free.

in the dream
there was no pain

for you
for me
for us

in the dream
i gave you love
and you put down your arms

in the dream
i gave you love
and you held it
and we had peace.

step outside.
see how the sun favors you.
i always see flowers
wanting to bloom in your eyes.
you are full of want.
you are buried beneath it.
your soft, tired heart
and your soft, tired soul
now just craves kindness.
i will bring it to you
so you can rest.
i will take you back to the tender garden
before you saw everything.
before you saw everything
you wanted to un-see.
you will plant your love back into the earth
and watch it grow.

there is a comfort
in watching things grow naturally.
there is a comfort in things that hold.

how beautiful you are
for never giving up on yourself,
for just waking up
and choosing to get out of bed.

seeing you own your life
and be so willing
to face it
over and over again
is so powerful,
you make me believe
anything is possible.

you make me believe
in heroes again.

i do not always know how to be brave.
i do not choose courage consistently,
but i always try to be truthful
in where i fail.

and i know
where i fail is where i need to begin.

it is where i will rise.

pay attention
   to what brings you close
   to the edge of your becoming.
that is where you belong.

it is there
where you'll finally see everything.

thank god we cannot escape
matters of the heart.
that no matter
how far we try to run away,
it finds its way to the front
and forces us to face it.

thank god our hearts do not stop
until we have listened to everything
it has to say.

i took a night drive.

i needed to get away.
i needed to know,
it's okay to go
and have no destination,
where time moves slow
or doesn't exist.
that life can be like this,
aimless wandering.
just breathing.
living.

driving forever
   underneath the stars.

the sky
blushing blue
for you.

the sky
hiding beneath the clouds
at the sound of your name.

the sky
shy and waiting
for you

to tell her
you love her
and it's going to be okay.

i will never push you away.
i know what that feels like.
i know what it's like to feel
  unwanted.
  unloved.
  out of place.

i know what it's like
to feel too much
and to feel like
you're always getting in your own way.

i will not add to that.
i will never make you feel like
  you are too much for your own skin.
i will never let you believe
  the whole world's against you.

when you reach for me,
i will not push you away.
i will give you my hand.

i will love you
i will love you
i will love you
always.

learn to accept the love
  you deserve.

here is my love for you.
it will be here for you always.

whenever you are ready.

be sad.
be so sad your heart cannot be sad anymore.
be so sad there's no sad for you left.

be sad enough to find the rest
   that is waiting for you.
be sad enough
   where there is an end.

you are not the story
they keep telling about you
over and over again.

you are not even the story
you keep telling yourself.

there are no lines
that can hold you.

there are not enough words
for all the more that you are.

on a tired street
in a house that is gutted
a bird still sings your name.

a bird
as yellow as the sun.

how lovely,
the way
the sky calls for you.

how pretty,
the way
she says your name.

tender was the throat i lived in.

i planted teeth in the front garden
so nothing that hasn't been made soft
would enter.

my forever lives in my mother.

she is the only one
i trust enough
to keep it safe.

my body houses scars
and loves them into flowers.

it took me much too long to learn
that we survive this life by forgiving.

start with yourself,
then with your father.

show me
all the parts of you
that you do not love

so i know where to begin.

i wish i could take your sadness
    away from you,
as if it was just something
    you could give away,
as if you could just cast it into the sky
and be done with it.

i don't really know what to do with you
when you are this sad,
and i know you don't know
what to do either,
but i am here.

i need you to know that i am here
and i am not going anywhere.

there's always been a little sadness
inside my happiness.

i've never been able
to separate the two.

my flesh, so soft—
    sadness seeps in
    and makes a home.

i feel everything.
i do not know how to un-feel
and to not feel
is to stop the sun.

i am
 like the moon—
  sometimes, full.
  sometimes, black.

  sometimes,
    forever and ever alone.

i sometimes think
i'm too in love with alone.

who could i love more
than this peace?

i took it off.
i did not want to
carry it with me anymore.

to remain soft
and to remain my own
is all i've ever wanted.

womxn.

woman—
another word for beginning.
another word for revolution.
another word for healing.
another word for being.
another word for me.

.

i am a woman
and i am alone,
and i cannot tell
which one of the two
i love being more.

there is a difference between
loneliness and solitude,
one will empty you
and
one will fill you.

you have the power to choose.

hold company with yourself so sacred
that even when you are alone,
   you are whole.

no one needs love from you
more than you need love from you.

love yourself first,
and you will always be in love.

your heart—
   soft
   and heavy with love.

your love—
   wild
   and warm like summer.

love is my thighs,
     this belly,
     my eyes.

love is my speech,
     the search,
     my cry.

love is myself in the mirror.
i will see love every time.

i bleed
  and the earth moves.
i bleed and it's spring.

it is new beginnings,
    new hope,
    new cells,
        red with purpose.

they always told me
i would go somewhere
and i would fall in love.

what they didn't know
was that i would go far
and i would fall in love with myself.

i didn't know how,
but i know now.

i know now
how to love
all the women in me.

i know now
how to love
myself deeply.

i know now
how to look in the mirror
and fall in love with the storm.

i am soft again.
there is water and it surrounds me.
there is feeling and i can feel it.

i am awake and alive
and swollen and heavy
with love.

i am changing
and i am loving change.

the woman is rain,
and when she falls,
she is a monsoon.

to love her is to drown.

the way the moon disappears
into the night
and comes back
full bright

that is what i'll do.

i am terrified of standing still,
of not moving,
of not being able to change.
i am terrified of staying the same.

what if this is all i have to offer?
what if there's nothing left for me to give?

these are the questions that haunt me
that lay with me in my bed.
these are the questions
that are still there when i wake
and stare at me straight in the eye.

i am not done.

i tell myself
i am not done.

i tell myself
over and over.

you love me
even when i can't love myself
and i can't thank you enough for that.

-    *mẹ ơi.*

(vietnamese, an affectionate call to my mother)

i never understood
competition between women.

to me, it's a lie
someone wants us to believe.

i love you.
you're beautiful.
look how beautiful we are
when we are together.

my strength should not threaten you.
my strength is not a threat to your strength.
   you are strong.
   you are beautiful.
   you are lush.
   you are powerful.
   as you are.
   as i am.

imagine the force we would be together
   if we lifted each other up.
imagine the force we would be together
   if we didn't tear each other down.

do not look at yourself
   through another's eyes.
their eyes hold
   prejudices and judgements
that have nothing to do with you
and everything to do with them.

look at yourself with kindness
and with truth.

you are
the prayer,
the poem,
the maker
and the made.

you are the seeker
and the gift.

you are everything.
and everything,
one in the same.

where they wanted rage,
i gave them kindness
and that changed everything.

be free
and be kind.

the only rules.

we do not heal
    by wounding another.
we become lost
        when we don't choose love.

we're all hurting
and we only show it in the ways
we know how.

pay
attention.

everything changes when you begin
to accept responsibility for your life,
when you begin to pay attention
to who you hurt,
to how you hurt,
to why you hurt.

and that when you do hurt,
    you are not alone.

when you pay attention,
you start to realize
  you can make the hurt change.
you start to realize
  how much power you do have
  and how much power you were giving away.
you start to realize how much time you have
been wasting.

this is when you take it all back—
    everything that is yours.
this is the beginning of everything.

you have been awakened.

when i finally saw my father
as a human being
and not the hero i always imagined,
that's when my healing began.

i have become protective
   of my energy.

i have learned how
   to let their energy
   pass through me

without sticking.
without hurting.
without me.

i'm at the point where
if you don't add to my life,
i will not sit here and wait
for you to leave.

i will open the door myself
and shut it hard behind me.

i am not waiting for you.

my life does not begin
        when you choose to come into my life.

i wait for no one.

my life begins
        when i choose to live it.

i will not hold my tongue
for your ego
or your comfort.

too many have fought
for my right to speak
and still so many
have not learned
how to listen.

i am no longer afraid.
nothing can bring me down lower
  than i have ever carried myself.
now, i tower
  over the ruin
  that was me.

now, i see the cocoon i built
  with these small hands.
i see the change
  that was meant for me.

i am this mystical being,
this brilliant light,
this ancient stardust.

now, i see.

there is nothing more powerful
than a woman in love

especially when she's in love with herself.

as i grow older,
i grow softer,
but this does not make me weak.

i grow softer
because i am braver.
  bolder.
bold enough to let it hurt me,
let you love me,
let universes
  inside of universes
  inside of me.

i grow softer
as i grow older
as i grow bolder.

this does not make me weak.

free.

i need to leave again.
i do not know how
   to stay in one place.

you want my heart,
   but my heart
      cannot be contained.

things and places do not keep me.

i have not found a home here
or here
or here.

my love is much
too broad
too wide
too hungry.

my love is much
too big
too mine
for here.

sometimes i can't believe
something so little as gravity
keeps my feet grounded,
keeps the wind from carrying me
across something so little as the sea.

i have left
so many beautiful places unfounded,
so many beautiful places yet to see.

go somewhere.
fall in love
and don't come back.

i was always the girl
who loved seeing the world
more than i loved being in love.
maybe i haven't found the right person,
maybe i was more in love with the world,
but if i were to choose between
being free or being in love,
i always choose to be free.

today:

today i'm going to hold onto joy
for as long as i can,
and when it goes,
it goes.

today i will be grateful
that i knew joy at all.

today
i put a note
in one of your pockets.

when you find it
it will tell you:

    you are beautiful
    you are loved
    you are seen
      right now
      i am thinking of you
      i am thinking of you always.

today is easy.

today,
someone calls your name
and you become soft.

you are in motion.
you are becoming.
you are growing soft
   and soft again,
like water—

new,
like spring.

today,
you are wanted.

today,
you belong.

things keep falling in and out of place.
this is the universe's way
of taking care of me.

how lovely it is
that i could just decide
   to be happy,
            that i could wake up
            and just own these words.

you giver of light.
you lover of love.

you
beautiful
beautiful
human being
you.

stay curious, love.

don't let the pain of the world
    close your eyes.

stay curious
and
stay
the brave,
strong,
unrelenting
soldier of love
that you are.

we get brave.
we move.
we believe.
we keep going.

AVA. currently lives in southern california. *you are safe here* is AVA.'s second book. her first book *this is how you know i want you* has been loved all over the world.

etsy.com/shop/AVApoetry
instagram.com/VAV.AVA
twitter.com/vav__ava
facebook.com/AVApoetry
vav-ava.tumblr.com
avapoet.wordpress.com
pinterest.com/AVAwriter

'all this writing has to lead to somewhere, right?'

'you think it'll lead you to the truth?'

'i don't think i'll ever know what the truth is. i just want to be free.'

31796451R00081

Made in the USA
San Bernardino, CA
20 March 2016